THIS BOOK
BELONGS TO:

_____

St. Thérèse

The Little Flower

Written by Alice Joyce Davidson
Illustrated by Maggie Swanson

Regina
Press

Thérèse Martin grew up in France.
She was the youngest of ten children.
Her mother died when she was very young.

Thérèse was a quiet girl and helpful
around the busy household.
But she had a secret wish.
She wanted to spend her life loving Jesus.

When she was only ten years old,
Thérèse became very ill with fever.

One night in her bedroom, she prayed for
healing to a statue of the Virgin Mary.
She saw the virgin smile at her!
The fever left instantly, and from
that day on, Thérèse knew the
power of prayer.

When she was fifteen, Thérèse
persuaded her father to allow her to
leave home and go to the Carmelite
convent in the town of Lisieux.
Her mission, she told her father,
was to help make God loved on earth.

At the convent, Thérèse began to write a journal. She wrote about her experiences of faith and what she was learning about God's love.

A daily task was to tend to the convent gardens. One day, as she was admiring the variety of beautiful flowers, she thought, "All the flowers God has created are so lovely, and so are all his people. He has created the great saints who are like lilies and roses, but He has also created ordinary people like us. We must be content to be the daisies and the violets which please His eyes whenever He glances down upon His earth."

Thérèse found ways to be content to live a simple life and become a Little Flower of Jesus. She prayed for others in secret and she taught the young nuns about the ways of the Lord.

She continued to write in her journal about the power of prayer and about finding heaven's beauty in the simple things around us.

From her journal:

"Lord Jesus,
I am not an eagle.
All I have are the eyes
and the heart of one.
In spite of my littleness,
I adore to gaze at the
sun of love
And long to fly
toward it"

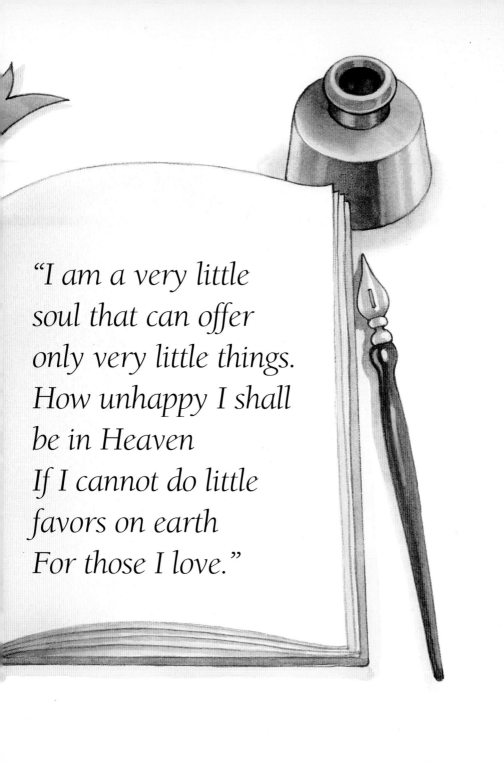

"I am a very little
soul that can offer
only very little things.
How unhappy I shall
be in Heaven
If I cannot do little
favors on earth
For those I love."

Though she was still very young, Saint Thérèse became ill, and her lungs began to fail. She would hide her pain with a smile, although her suffering was enormous. When she knew she was dying, she told her friends and family, "Pray to me, and I will answer you with a shower of roses."

After she died, her journal, "The Story of A Soul" was published. It became so popular that she was called a "hurricane of glory." She became a saint in 1925.

Today when people pray to Saint Thérèse, The Little Flower, they often speak of seeing or smelling roses - a sign to them that their prayers will be answered!